Drawing Conclusions

The Jamestown Comprehension Skills Series with Writing Activities

THIRD EDITION

JAMESTOWN  PUBLISHERS

a division of NTC/Contemporary Publishing Group
Lincolnwood, Illinois USA

ISBN: 0-8092-0236-0

Published by Jamestown Publishers,
a division of NTC/Contemporary Publishing Group, Inc.
©2000 NTC/Contemporary Publishing Group, Inc.,
4255 West Touhy Avenue, Lincolnwood Illinois 60712-1975 U.S.A.

5 6 7 8 9 10 11 12 117 09 08 07 06 05

INTRODUCTION

The Comprehension Skills Series has been prepared to help students develop specific reading comprehension skills. Each book is completely self-contained. There is no separate answer key or instruction manual. Throughout the book, clear and concise directions guide the student through the lessons and exercises.

The titles of the Comprehension Skills books match the labels found on comprehension questions in other Jamestown textbooks. The student who is having difficulty with a particular kind of question can use the matching Comprehension Skills book for extra instruction and practice to correct the specific weakness.

Each book in the Comprehension Skills Series is divided into five parts.

1. Explanation: Part One (p. 5) clearly defines, explains, and illustrates the specific skill. It begins with a Preview Quiz to get students thinking about the material that will be presented.

2. Instruction: Part Two (p. 8) offers an interesting and informative lesson presented in clear, readable language. This section also utilizes the preview technique introduced in Part One, which requires students to anticipate and respond to the subject matter.

3. Sample Exercise: Part Three (p. 17) consists of a sample exercise with questions. The sample exercise is designed to prepare students for the work required in the following section. Students should read and follow the instructions carefully. When they have finished the exercise, they should read the analysis following it. For each question, there is a step-by-step explanation of why one answer is correct, and why the others are not. Students are urged to consult the teacher if they need extra help before proceeding to Part Four.

4. Practice Exercises: Part Four (p. 23) contains twenty practice exercises with questions. Squares (■) bordering the exercises indicate the level of difficulty. The greater the number of squares, the greater the difficulty of the passage. Students are advised to read the instructions and complete the practice exercises thoughtfully and carefully.

5. Writing Activities: Part Five (p. 49) contains writing activities that help students apply the skills they have learned in earlier parts of the book. Students should read and follow the instructions carefully. Many activities encourage students to work together cooperatively. The teacher may want to discuss these activities in class.

Each book also contains an Answer Key, which can be found after the Writing Activities. Students can record their scores and monitor their progress on the chart following the Answer Key.

Understanding Conclusions

As a preview of Part One, try to complete this sentence:

A conclusion is a decision about

  a. what may happen.

  b. what may have caused something.

  c. how believable an argument is.

Begin reading Part One to find the correct answer.

Conclusions Defined

What is a conclusion? It's a decision about what may happen. It's a decision about the result an event may have.

Suppose you saw clouds in the sky. Then you felt the wind pick up. You heard thunder in the distance. You ran inside. Why?

You drew a conclusion. You concluded that rain was coming. You saw clouds, felt wind, heard thunder. Those were the facts. You asked yourself, "What may happen? What will result from these facts?" "Rain!" you answered.

Why You Must Draw Your Own Conclusions

Writers often mean more than they say. They do not state everything they want you to understand. They leave things out, even important things.

Sometimes, for instance, they don't state conclusions. They want you to draw them. Why do authors make you draw your own conclusions? They may have several reasons.

- They may think that the result is obvious. They think everyone will know it. It doesn't have to be said.

- They want *you* to find the result. The writer leads you toward it and then stops. Now you're on your own. If *you* draw the conclusion, you will be more likely to believe it's right.

- The writer's purpose for writing may differ from your reason for reading. The conclusions may not suit the writer's purpose.

Reasonable Conclusions

Conclusions may be missing from the things you read. You may have to draw your own. Only then can you be sure that you understand what you have read.

Let's see what reasonable conclusions are. First read this passage.

> Heavy rains have continued upstate. The Blackstone River is rising quickly. It should crest Tuesday night. Towns along the banks are sure to be flooded. Power is likely to be cut off.

A good reader can draw many conclusions from the facts. The reader asks, "What are the facts? What may result from them? What do they imply?"

- *Heavy rains have continued upstate.*
  The rain may cause floods.

- *The Blackstone River is rising quickly.*
  The river may overflow its banks.

- *It should crest Tuesday night.*
  That is the most dangerous time. People should act before then.

- *Towns along the banks are sure to be flooded.*
  People should leave those towns.

- *Power is likely to be cut off.*
  People should have candles and flashlights ready.

Those are reasonable conclusions. They were drawn from the facts.

PART TWO

Drawing a Conclusion

Preview Quiz 2

As a preview of Part Two, try to answer this question:

How are causes and effects related?

   a. They are not related.

   b. Effects make causes happen.

   c. Causes make effects happen.

Begin reading Part Two to find the answer.

Causes and Effects

How can you draw a conclusion? Start with causes and effects. Much of our thinking is based on causes and effects. Life shows us that some things cause others. That is, one event makes another happen.

You eat an ice-cream cone on a hot day. The heat melts the ice cream. It drips down your arm. The heat is the cause. The drip is the effect.

The drip stains your shirt. This time, the drip is the cause. The stain is the effect. A dripping cone causes a stained shirt.

8

How Writers State Causes and Effects

There are many ways to state causes and effects. A writer may use any of the following ways:

Because the weather is hot, the ice cream drips.
The weather is hot. Therefore, the ice cream drips.
If the weather is hot, then the ice cream will drip.

If the ice cream drips on your shirt, it will stain the shirt.

Missing Effects

Writers may leave the effects out. They may only state the cause. They ask you to decide the effect.

You sometimes do that, too. You might say to a friend, "Watch out. Your cone is dripping!" You state the cause: a dripping cone. You don't state the effect: a stained shirt. Your friend has to draw a conclusion. He or she wonders, "What does that fact imply? What will result from a dripping cone?"

Again, your first step in drawing a conclusion is to find causes and effects. Look for causes. Decide what effects they imply. Find the causes in this passage.

Native Alaskans used to live on what they hunted and caught. They traded with neighbors for things they needed.

These are causes. The writer hasn't stated their effects. You can figure them out. Try saying to yourself, "If . . . then . . ."

If people lived on what they hunted and caught, *then* . . .

If people traded with neighbors for things they needed, *then* . . .

You should see the effect. They wouldn't need money. Once native Alaskans didn't need money.

Read this passage.

> Today native Alaskan people need gas for their snowmobiles. They need oil to heat their homes. They order down coats from catalogs. They buy stereos and televisions.

Can you see the effect? Try the *if . . . then . . .* technique. You should see that Alaskan people now need to use money.

Preview Quiz 3

Try to finish this statement:

What you read may suggest many conclusions. You should consider all of them. ***Then you can***

   a.   pick any conclusion you like.

   b.   decide which conclusion is most likely.

   c.   ignore the other facts.

Continue reading to find the answer.

Think While You Read

Good readers think while they read. They consider the ideas. They weigh statements. They try to decide where facts lead. They think about what the passage implies, or suggests.

Good readers keep an open mind. They do not jump to conclusions. Instead, they wait. They think about their reading. They consider all the conclusions. Then they settle on the most likely ones.

You, too, should think about all the conclusions before choosing one. Why? One cause may have several effects. So one set of facts may lead to several conclusions. By thinking about all of the conclusions, you can decide which one is best.

An Example

The next paragraph will show you why you should consider all the conclusions. The paragraph is about ducks. As you read, watch for causes. Think about effects they may have.

Most ducks have light, hollow bones. Light bones make it easier for ducks that feed on the surface of the water to stay afloat. Diving ducks, however, often chase fish under water. Diving ducks have much heavier bones than surface-feeding ducks.

Many statements in the paragraph are causes. Each cause implies certain effects. Here are two causes.

Most ducks have light, hollow bones.
Diving ducks have heavy bones.

What effects do those causes imply? Try the *if. . . then . . .* technique.

If most ducks have light, hollow bones, *then . . .*
If diving ducks have heavy bones, *then . . .*

Think of as many effects as you can. Make a list of the effects. Save your list. Now find causes in this paragraph.

Most drakes (male ducks) are brightly colored. However, at the end of the mating season most drakes molt. That is, they lose their old feathers. Without their flight feathers, the drakes are unable to fly. They also lose their bright coloring and turn a dull brown.

Did you find these causes?

Most drakes are brightly colored.
Drakes can't fly when they lose their old feathers.
The drakes turn a dull brown when they molt.

What effects do those causes imply? Again, try the *if . . . then . . .* technique. Think of as many effects as you can. List them. Save the list. You will need your lists in the next section.

Preview Quiz 4

Try to answer this question:

All the parts of a paragraph are related. This includes the causes and effects. *How are they related?*

   a. They are not related.

   b. Each stands alone.

   c. They work together.

Continue reading to find the answer.

Causes and Effects in Paragraphs

The parts of a paragraph work together. The details develop a topic. They are about one main idea. Causes and effects work together too. They may lead to one main conclusion. Let's see how this works. In the last section, you found causes in paragraphs about ducks. You listed the possible effects. We'll start with the first paragraph. We'll use the *if . . . then . . .* technique. You may have these effects on your list.

If most ducks have light, hollow bones,
then they float very well.
    They can swim quickly.
    They can feed on the surface of the water.

If diving ducks have heavy bones,
then they can swim under water.
    They can chase fish under water.

Think about these effects. You should begin to see a pattern. What can you conclude from these facts?

> *If* ducks with light bones float very well,
> *then* heavy bones must help diving ducks catch fish under water.

The causes and effects work together. They lead to one main conclusion.

Now let's look at the second paragraph. Your list may have these effects.

> *If* most drakes are brightly colored,
> *then* they are pretty.
> **They are easy to see.**

> *If* drakes are unable to fly when they molt,
> *then* they cannot travel far.
> **They cannot escape easily from enemies.**

> *If* drakes turn a dull brown when they molt,
> *then* they are not as pretty.
> **They are harder to see.**

Again, you should see a pattern. Some effects are more important. They are in boldfaced type. What do those facts imply?

> *If* drakes without all their feathers can't escape easily from their enemies, but are harder to see with dull brown feathers, *then* drakes can easily hide from their enemies when they molt.

Now you can see why you should consider all the likely conclusions. Keep an open mind. Consider all the possibilities. Then draw a conclusion. Look for one main conclusion.

Preview Quiz 5

Try to answer this question:

What is the best test of a conclusion?

   a. Is it interesting?

   b. Does it make sense?

   c. Does the writer state it?

Continue reading to find the answer.

When the Conclusion Is the Main Idea

You know that:

- writers do not always state their main ideas
- you sometimes have to draw your own conclusions

Sometimes the conclusion *is* the main idea. But it isn't stated. The whole passage points toward it. But no one sentence states it. You find it by looking at all the facts. See what each implies. Draw one conclusion from all of them. Then test it.

How can you test it? See whether it makes sense. Making sense is the best test of a conclusion.

Try it with this passage.

What happens in an eclipse of the moon? To find out, let's imagine an "eclipse of the cat." Suppose that you are standing in the sun. You cast a shadow. Now suppose a cat is walking around you. You turn to watch it as it walks. Sometimes the cat walks into your shadow. You can see your shadow cover more and more of the cat. At one point, all of the cat is in shadow. This is a full eclipse of the cat. Earth is lit by the sun, too. The moon goes around Earth, just as the cat goes around you. Sometimes the entire moon is in the shadow.

The main idea is not stated. Nor is the main conclusion stated. But some facts in the passage lead to conclusions. Here are some facts. Their conclusions follow them.

Fact: Earth is lit by the sun, too.
Conclusion: Earth casts a shadow, as you do.

Fact: The moon goes around Earth, just as the cat goes around you.
Conclusion: Sometimes the moon passes into Earth's shadow.

Fact: Sometimes the entire moon is in the shadow.
Conclusion: This is a full eclipse of the moon.

Now you can see the man idea. Now you can draw the main conclusion. It is:

In a full eclipse, the moon passes entirely into Earth's shadow.

Summary

Draw conclusions as you read. Follow these steps.

- Watch for causes. What effects could they have? Use the *if . . . then . . .* technique.

- Stretch your thinking. Don't stop with the obvious effects. Try to imagine all possible conclusions. One cause may have many effects. One set of facts may lead to many conclusions.

- Keep an open mind. Put your findings together.

- Draw your conclusions. Do they make sense? Making sense is the best test.

PART THREE

Sample Exercise

On the next page is a sample exercise. It shows how to use what you have learned in Parts One and Two.

The sample also previews the twenty exercises in Part Four. Read the sample passage and answer the sample questions. That will get you off to a good start.

The answers to the questions are explained. You will find out why the correct answers are the best answers. You will see where the wrong answers are faulty. The text also tells how you might think as you work through the exercise correctly.

Finish the sample carefully. Give it some thought. Do not go on to Part Four until you are sure you understand how to draw conclusions.

____ Sample Exercise _____

While he was president, Grover Cleveland had a secret operation. A doctor discovered a lump on Cleveland's jaw. Tests showed that the lump was cancerous.

Cleveland left the White House suddenly. His staff announced that he would be on vacation for a month. He took a train to New York. Then he boarded a friend's yacht. That night on the yacht, four doctors operated on him.

The president rested for a few weeks. Meanwhile, Americans thought their president was enjoying a long vacation. Then newspapers reported that President Cleveland was very ill. Rumors began to spread. The White House denied the rumors. Finally, Cleveland himself stopped the rumors. He appeared in public at last. Reporters carefully watched him for any sign of illness. They found the president in excellent health.

1. The lump was cancerous. Doctors concluded that
   a. there was no reason to worry.
   b. Cleveland should take a vacation.
   c. they had to operate at once.
   d. the newspapers should be told.

2. The public concluded that Cleveland was on vacation. Which fact supported that conclusion?
   a. Cleveland boarded a friend's yacht.
   b. Cleveland had been examined by doctors.
   c. Newspapers reported that he was ill.
   d. Cleveland left the White House suddenly.

3. The main idea suggests the conclusion that Cleveland
   a. took long vacations while he was president.
   b. was never really ill.
   c. often lied to the press.
   d. thought people might panic if they knew he was ill.

4. Someone may have "leaked" the truth to a reporter. Underline a sentence that supports this conclusion.

Answers and Explanations

1. To finish this sentence, think about causes and effects. You are given the cause. You must choose the effect. Read each possible effect. Which would result because the lump was cancerous?

The best answer is *c*. The doctors had to operate at once.

Answer *a* is wrong. It is the opposite of the truth. All the events happened because the doctors had to operate. They had to act quickly.

Answer *b* is wrong. A vacation can't cure cancer. The vacation was just an excuse. It hid the cancer from the public.

Answer *d* is wrong. Cleveland and his staff tried to hide the illness. The doctors would not come to that conclusion either. They were worried about Cleveland's health. They weren't thinking about news.

2. Now you must find a cause. The question gives you the effect—the conclusion. What fact leads to it? Use the *if . . . then . . .* technique. Try to think as the public did.

If (something), *then* Cleveland must be on vacation.
Try each cause after *if.* See which makes sense.

The best answer is *a.* A yacht is a fine place for a vacation. No one would expect an operation to take place there.

Answer *b* is wrong. Seeing a doctor doesn't suggest that a person is going on a vacation.

Answer *c* is wrong. A report of illness doesn't suggest a vacation.

Answer *d* is wrong. Leaving the White House suddenly suggests an emergency.

3. First decide what the main idea is. The passage leads to the idea that Cleveland didn't want people to know that he was ill.

The best answer is *d*. Cleveland thought people might panic if they knew he was ill.

Answer *a* is wrong. The vacation was only a trick. Nothing in the passage suggests that Cleveland really took long vacations.

Answer *b* is wrong. We are told that he was really ill. The doctors had to operate.

Answer *c* is wrong. Cleveland misled the press in this case. But we don't know *from this passage* that he ever did again.

4. You must find a sentence that supports a conclusion. The sentence must be the cause of an effect. Review the paragraph. Look for a likely cause. Use the *if . . . then . . .* technique.

If (something), *then* someone must have "leaked" the truth to a reporter.

The best answer is this sentence.

> Then newspapers reported that President Cleveland was very ill.

Did you have trouble answering these questions correctly? If so, read the sample exercise and questions again. If you still don't understand the answers and the reasons for them, check with your teacher before going on.

PART FOUR

Practice Exercises

- The twenty exercises that follow will help you use your ability to draw conclusions.

- Each exercise is like the sample in Part Three.

- Read each passage well. Answer the questions carefully and thoughtfully.

- Correct your answers using the Answer Key at the back of the book. Mark your scores on the chart on page 64 before going on to the next exercise.

Practice Exercise 1

Hyattsville, Maryland, is near Washington, D.C. Back in the 1920s, the public-school football team had a possum as a mascot. One day it disappeared. The whole team was upset. Students looked everywhere. They couldn't find it. At the same time, a possum was found on the White House grounds. President Hoover adopted it. A photo of the possum was in all the papers.

The students thought that the president had their possum. Some of them went to the White House to see the possum. It was kept in the kennels. It would not come out. All the students could do was leave a note. They asked that the possum take the place of the one they had lost. The president ordered the possum delivered to the team at once.

The team had its mascot back. Hyattsville went on to play in the state championship series.

1. The students concluded that the president had their possum. Which fact supports that?
   a. Their possum disappeared one day.
   b. His possum was found when theirs disappeared.
   c. The whole team was upset.
   d. The White House possum was kept in the kennels.

2. President Hoover gave the possum to the students. You can conclude that he
   a. sympathized with them.
   b. didn't like possums.
   c. had absolute proof that it was theirs.
   d. was a great football fan.

3. Which conclusion does the main idea suggest?
   a. Possums bring good luck.
   b. President Hoover loved pets.
   c. Possums should not be kept in kennels.
   d. The team's spirits rose when they got the possum back.

4. Someone gave the students' note to the president. Underline the sentence that supports that conclusion.

Practice Exercise **2**

Most people know of the California Gold Rush of 1849. Thousands of people streamed to the West. Each hoped to strike it rich. They panned for gold in rivers, and they dug for it in the hills. Some people got rich. Others were disappointed.

Not many people know of the Vermont Gold Rush. One man who didn't strike it rich out West came home to Vermont. He was determined to find gold! In 1851, he found it in a brook near Plymouth. At the time, the brook was called Buffalo Brook, but soon its name was changed to Gold Brook!

For forty years, miners worked that brook. They panned, washed, and dug out the gold. One mining company claimed to have found two thousand dollars' worth of gold there daily.

People still go to Gold Brook today. Some take their pans, dreaming of great wealth. Others take their picnic baskets and enjoy the view.

1. Few people have heard of the Vermont Gold Rush. You can conclude that
a. it was famous the world over.
b. it was much smaller than the California Gold Rush.
c. people pretended that it never happened.
d. the government kept it secret.

2. If people can find gold in some rivers and brooks, then
a. rain must wash gold out of the soil.
b. there must be gold all over North America.
c. anyone can get rich by panning for gold.
d. gold may be a health hazard.

3. Which conclusion does the main idea suggest?
a. People are still making a fortune from Gold Brook.
b. Vermont is about the same size as California.
c. There isn't much gold left in Gold Brook today.
d. Gold isn't valuable now.

4. You can conclude that Gold Brook is a pretty spot. Underline the sentence that supports that conclusion.

Practice Exercise 3

The first drive-in movie theater opened at the height of the Depression. Films were popular then. They helped people forget their problems. People liked the idea of the drive-in. A car full of folks could get in for just one dollar per car. On the drive-in movie's opening night, six hundred people came.

Sound was a problem. At first, sound came from speakers in the ground. Cars parked over them. The sound was supposed to come through the floorboards. But it didn't come through very well. New large speakers were placed beside the screen. Then all the people in the drive-in could hear the sound. All the people in the neighborhood could hear it, too. The owners had to find another solution. In time, a speaker was hung inside each car window.

1. Six hundred people came on opening night. You can conclude that
   a. the cost of a movie was too expensive.
   b. people were excited about color movies.
   c. the Depression cost many people their jobs.
   d. the first drive-in was a success.

2. People near the drive-in complained about the large speakers. Which fact supports that conclusion?
   a. The owners had to find another solution.
   b. The speakers were placed near the screen.
   c. Everyone in the drive-in could hear the sound.
   d. The speakers in the ground were replaced.

3. The drive-in cost one dollar per car. You can conclude that
   a. six hundred cars arrived on opening night.
   b. a person could see a movie for less than a dollar.
   c. films were popular then.
   d. people liked the idea of watching movies from their cars.

4. Not much sound comes through the bottom of a car. Underline the sentence that supports that conclusion.

Practice Exercise 4

Snakes and lizards are reptiles. Reptiles are cold-blooded animals. The temperature of their blood changes with the weather. When the air is warm, their blood is warm, too. When the air is cold, the temperature of their blood goes down. If the reptiles get too cold, they may die. They must find a protected place when the days are cold. They may stay in holes under the ground. They may stay in caves. Or they may find a place under rotting tree stumps. Even in those protected spots, the reptiles are too cold to move. They lie still until the air warms up. Then they come back outside.

1. Snakes and lizards are reptiles. You can conclude that
   a. they are active all year round.
   b. they stay out of caves.
   c. their blood temperature changes.
   d. cold does not affect them.

2. In winter, a reptile without shelter
   a. is likely to die.
   b. enjoys cold days most.
   c. becomes warm-blooded.
   d. eats more than usual.

3. Which conclusion about cold-blooded animals does the main idea suggest?
   a. They change their temperature as they wish.
   b. They suffer in hot climates.
   c. They are most active in the winter.
   d. They cannot keep their blood at one temperature.

4. Underline the sentence that supports the conclusion in number 2.

┌─ Practice Exercise **5** ─────────────────────

Glaciers are great sheets of ice on land. They move very slowly. In many places in the far north and the far south they reach the sea. The ice pushes past the edge of the water. Then huge pieces break off and float away. Those pieces are called icebergs.

Iceberg means "mountain of ice." An iceberg can be many miles wide and as tall as a fifty-story building. Only about one-ninth of the iceberg is visible above the water. The hidden bulk may spread out into a great shelf of ice.

One of the worst shipwrecks of all time was caused by an iceberg. In 1912, the *Titanic* began its first voyage. It was the biggest passenger ship ever built. In the North Sea, it struck a hidden iceberg. It sank, and more than fifteen hundred lives were lost.

1. Which conclusion does the main idea of the first paragraph suggest?
   a. Icebergs drift as far as the equator.
   b. Most icebergs melt quickly.
   c. Iceland is actually a huge iceberg.
   d. Icebergs begin on land as glaciers.

2. Which conclusion does the main idea of the second paragraph suggest?
   a. Most of an iceberg is below the water.
   b. Icebergs are tall and narrow like skyscrapers.
   c. In cold areas, the ocean bottom is ice.
   d. Ice forms in thin layers.

3. The hidden part of an iceberg may spread out over a great distance. You can conclude that
   a. it is safe to sail close to one.
   b. ships should stay far away from icebergs.
   c. icebergs tip easily.
   d. fish find rich feeding grounds beneath icebergs.

4. You can conclude that icebergs look like mountains. Underline the sentence that supports that conclusion.

— Practice Exercise **6** ——————————

Baseball in its early days was different from the game that's played today.

Years ago, umpires tried almost *too* hard to be fair. Before they made calls, they would stop the game to hear testimony from the players. They would then ask the opinion of the fans. Finally, they would make their calls.

Catchers were less protected then. They had no chest protectors. They had no masks. They had no shin guards.

Batters played a different role then, too. They could call to the pitcher for a high or low ball. They also had to take nine balls instead of four before walking to first base.

Today the pitcher's mound is sixty feet (about 18 meters) from the batter. But the pitcher used to stand only thirty-five feet (about 11 meters) away from the batter.

1. The pitcher's mound was closer then. You can conclude that
  a. pitchers had to throw harder then.
  b. catchers were less important then.
  c. batters had to react more quickly then.
  d. pitchers are more important now.

2. There were probably fewer arguments over an umpire's call then. Which paragraph supports that conclusion?
  a. paragraph one
  b. paragraph two
  c. paragraph four
  d. paragraph five

3. Which conclusion does paragraph three suggest?
  a. A team needed fewer pitchers then.
  b. Catchers are better trained now.
  c. Batters stood in a different spot then.
  d. Catchers were injured more often then.

4. Pitchers walked fewer batters in the old days than now. Underline the sentence that supports that conclusion.

Practice Exercise 7

Thomas Hobson lived more than three hundred years ago. He owned an inn and a stable of horses. His horses were for rent. Most people wanted to pick the best horses to rent. Hobson didn't want the horses to be worn out. He wanted to be sure they had a good rest after they had been ridden. So he came up with a plan. When a person wanted a horse, Hobson gave no choice. The person had to take the horse in the stall nearest the stable door. If the person wouldn't take that horse, he or she got no horse at all.

When someone brought a horse back, Hobson put it into the stall farthest from the door. When a horse went out, he moved each horse one stall closer to the door.

We have an expression today called "Hobson's choice." What do you suppose it means? It means a situation in which you have no choice.

1. You can conclude that Hobson's horses
   a. were quickly worn out.
   b. were rented most of the time.
   c. were rented for a much lower price than other horses.
   d. each got about the same amount of work.

2. You can conclude that the horse nearest the stable door
   a. was worn out soonest.
   b. had had the longest rest.
   c. had just come back from being rented.
   d. was the best horse in the stable.

3. You can conclude that "Hobson's choice" means
   a. "pick your own."
   b. "take it or leave it."
   c. "the customer is always right."
   d. "everyone likes a bargain."

4. Hobson concluded that the best horses would be worn out if he let people choose. Underline the sentence that supports that conclusion.

Practice Exercise *8*

Comedian Groucho Marx loved to play golf. However, on his best days he never broke the score of ninety. Top players score in the sixties. One day, playing in Boston, he got lucky. He took a mighty swipe at the ball and got a hole-in-one. The *Boston Globe* wrote about Groucho's success. It also printed three photos. Groucho's picture was in the middle. On either side were Bobby Jones and Walter Hagen. Underneath was the caption "Groucho Joins the Immortals."

Groucho resumed play the next day. When he came to the hole that he had made in one shot, he fell apart. He hacked and whacked away, but he took twenty two shots to sink the ball. The *Boston Globe* reported this, too. They also reprinted pictures of Jones and Hagen. Between the pictures, they left a blank spot. This time the caption read, "Groucho Leaves the Immortals."

1. From the way the *Boston Globe* handled the story, you can conclude that
   a. the *Boston Globe* editors didn't like Groucho.
   b. the *Boston Globe* editors didn't know much about golf.
   c. the *Boston Globe* editors were kidding Groucho.
   d. Groucho had once been a reporter for the *Boston Globe*.

2. Which fact supports the conclusion that Bobby Jones and Walter Hagen were famous golf stars?
   a. The *Boston Globe* called them "immortals."
   b. Groucho equaled their best scores.
   c. They had refused to play with Groucho.
   d. They had never gotten a hole-in-one.

3. Which conclusion does the main idea suggest?
   a. Groucho's golf game was improving daily.
   b. Groucho wasn't likely to repeat his golfing success.
   c. Walter Hagen would no longer be famous.
   d. The *Boston Globe* decided to expand its sports coverage.

4. In golf, a lower score is better. Underline the two sentences that support that conclusion.

Practice Exercise 9

The earliest people found food by hunting and gathering. First they used clubs and stones. Later they used bows and arrows, spears, and other weapons. They roamed the forests in search of wild animals. They dug into the earth for edible roots. They gathered wild berries, fruits, and nuts from the meadows and valleys. They spent most of their time gathering food. Their main job was feeding themselves.

People made an important discovery when they began farming. A spring planting meant a fall harvest that furnished food to last through the winter. Raising and breeding animals meant an adequate supply of meat. Life was changing. People began forming villages and communities. They shared their harvest and knowledge of farming. For a long time people had merely survived. Now they had time to spend on art and culture. Life became more pleasant and meaningful.

1. The earliest people spent most of their time hunting and gathering. You can conclude that they
a. ate well.
b. began to develop music and art.
c. lived in settled communities.
d. had little time for art and culture.

2. The author concludes that people formed villages so that they could
a. hunt together.
b. work together to produce more food.
c. protect themselves from wild animals.
d. form groups to gather berries, fruits, and nuts.

3. Which conclusion does the main idea suggest?
a. Farming gave people time for other things.
b. People were better off as hunters and gatherers.
c. Edible roots are important to our health.
d. Hunting animals is cruel.

4. Underline the sentence that supports the conclusion in number 2.

—— Practice Exercise *10* ——

Ludwig II ruled Bavaria in the late nineteenth century. Some people say he was a great king. Others say he was insane and wasteful.

Ludwig's father didn't believe that kings should go to school. Ludwig spent his youth at home with his mother and servants. He read poems and enjoyed music. He studied the paintings on the castle walls. He became quiet and spent a lot of time alone.

When Ludwig was eighteen, his father died. Ludwig became king. He knew nothing of politics. He was a strange king. He helped the great composer Richard Wagner get started. He built fancy castles for himself. He built schools for his people. He collected great art. He spent much of Bavaria's gold doing those things.

Other powers waged war on Bavaria. Ludwig wasn't prepared to lead his people in war. Bavaria suffered. War and poverty spread throughout the land.

1. Because Ludwig's father didn't believe in school for kings,
  a. Ludwig wasn't prepared to rule Bavaria.
  b. Ludwig studied war with great generals.
  c. Ludwig taught himself history.
  d. Richard Wagner tutored Ludwig in music.

2. Which fact supports the conclusion that Ludwig was wasteful?
  a. He wasn't prepared to lead in war.
  b. He built schools for his people.
  c. He built fancy castles for himself.
  d. He had no real education.

3. Which conclusion can you draw about Ludwig?
  a. He was the worst thing that ever happened to Bavaria.
  b. He did great things for his people.
  c. He had more talent than people give him credit for.
  d. He had good and bad points.

4. Some people say Ludwig was a great king. Underline a sentence that supports that conclusion.

— Practice Exercise *11* —————————————————

The red squirrel is found in Alaska, western Canada, and the northwestern states of the United States. Unlike gray squirrels, red squirrels do not bury their food in the ground. But like all squirrels, they do not hibernate. In the fall, red squirrels hide their food at the bases of trees and among roots. They link their pantries with tunnels beneath the snow. In winter, they seldom go far from these hidden pantries. The red squirrel spends more time around pine trees than other squirrels do. They are sometimes called pine squirrels. Red squirrels store cones as well as nuts for food. It is easy to spot a red squirrel's nest. They like to line their nests with strips of cedar bark when they can find it. Red squirrels are smaller than gray squirrels. They are probably the noisiest of all squirrels.

1. You can conclude that *gray* squirrels
   a. are noisier than red squirrels.
   b. hibernate.
   c. spend most of their time in pine trees.
   d. bury their food in the ground.

2. Red squirrels remember where they hide their food. Which fact supports that conclusion?
   a. They line their nests with cedar bark.
   b. They spend a lot of time near pine trees.
   c. They link their pantries with snow tunnels.
   d. They sometimes hide their food among roots.

3. You can conclude that you are likely to see *red* squirrels in a
   a. pine forest in Alaska.
   b. park in Quebec.
   c. field in Virginia.
   d. swamp in Florida.

4. Red squirrels are sometimes called pine squirrels. Underline the sentence that states the cause for that statement.

Practice Exercise *12*

Someone has said that you are a monotone or that you sing off-key. Now you think that you can't sing. Don't you believe it. A monotone is a singer who sings everything on one note. If you're a monotone, you have trouble distinguishing between high and low pitches. It doesn't mean that you *can't* sing different pitches. It only means that you have to learn how to do it. A real monotone probably talks on the same pitch, too. Try talking for five minutes without letting your voice go higher or lower. It will naturally try to go up and down. Put your hand on your neck. Feel your neck muscles working when you talk. You control the pitch. Your voice can do the same thing when you sing. You must listen very carefully and make it go higher or lower to the right degree at the right time.

1. People control pitch when they talk. The author concludes that most people
   a. speak in a monotone.
   b. can learn to control pitch when they sing.
   c. sing on the same pitch, too.
   d. can't sing different pitches.

2. Throat muscles control pitch. Which statement suggests that conclusion?
   a. A real monotone talks on the same pitch.
   b. A monotone sings everything on one note.
   c. Monotones can't tell high pitches from low pitches.
   d. Your neck muscles work when you talk.

3. Which conclusion does the main idea suggest?
   a. You can sing if you learn to control your voice.
   b. Monotones cannot learn to control pitch.
   c. Most singers begin as monotones.
   d. To sing well, you must first learn to talk in a monotone.

4. Underline the sentence that states the cause that makes "you" conclude that you can't sing.

Practice Exercise *13*

The *New York World* had the first newspaper comic strip. It appeared in 1894. It was printed in full color. The *World*'s rival paper was the *Morning Journal*. When the *World*'s comic strip came out, the *Journal* had to do something better. It printed a weekly comics section. This was the first of the "Sunday funnies."

The comics competition had begun! Soon the *Journal* started a new feature. It was a daily strip called "The Yellow Kid." This was the first strip with a story that continued each day. It's famous for something else, too. It was the first strip to use speech balloons.

By 1904, many papers ran daily strips. To cut costs, they appeared in black and white. One of the most popular was called "Mr. A. Mutt." Over the years it changed to "Mutt and Jeff." It is still widely read today.

1. The *Journal* felt that it had to compete with the *World*'s comic strip. You can conclude that
a. the *World*'s strip was not successful.
b. there was not much news in 1894.
c. the *Journal* had many more readers than the *World*.
d. the *World*'s strip increased sales.

2. "The Yellow Kid" was more like modern strips than the *World*'s strip was. Which fact supports that conclusion?
a. It used speech balloons.
b. It appeared in the *Morning Journal*.
c. It was printed in full color.
d. It appeared before "Mr. A. Mutt."

3. Which conclusion does the main idea suggest?
a. Comics never really succeeded in newspapers.
b. Some people buy a paper because of the comics.
c. "Mutt and Jeff" was the most popular strip.
d. "The Yellow Kid" was the first comic strip.

4. In printing, color costs more than black and white. Underline the sentence that supports that conclusion.

— Practice Exercise **14** —

In 1971, a young woman reporter was hired by a large city paper. She had a master's degree in journalism. She had worked for four years on a large school paper. She had spent two years writing for a wire service. She had covered hard news. Still, her editors gave her only "safe stories" with no daily deadlines. She was never sent out on a "breaking story."

One day, the city got a call. A grisly crime had just occurred downtown. The editor searched the newsroom. All the men were out to lunch. He had to send the woman reporter. She turned in the story well before deadline. Surprised, the editor said, "Hmmm, this isn't bad!" Today that woman *is* the editor. She employs three times as many women as her editor did. She sends them out on all kinds of news stories, no matter how grisly.

1. The editors gave the reporter only "safe stories." You can conclude that they believed she was
   a. overqualified.
   b. not capable.
   c. eager.
   d. fully trained.

2. The main idea of the first paragraph suggests this conclusion: The editor didn't send the reporter on "breaking stories" because she
   a. was a woman.
   b. wasn't well educated.
   c. didn't have enough experience.
   d. had only written about "soft" news.

3. The main idea of the second paragraph suggests this conclusion: The reporter
   a. failed miserably at her first tough assignment.
   b. had to find an easier job.
   c. proved that a woman could do the job.
   d. caused the editor to lose his job.

4. Luck gave the reporter a chance to prove herself. Underline a sentence that supports that conclusion.

—— Practice Exercise 1**5** ——

Those who knew Abraham Lincoln said he was a man of many faces. When he was silent, he often seemed sad and gloomy. But when he began to speak, his expression changed. "The dull features dropped like a mask," said one reporter. "The eyes began to sparkle. The mouth began to smile. A stranger would have said, 'Why, this man is really handsome!' "

Lincoln was the most photographed man of his time. His friends insisted that no photo ever did him justice. Lincoln looks very stiff and formal in his photos. We never see him laughing or joking. It's no wonder. Back then, cameras required long exposures. The person photographed had to "freeze" as the seconds ticked by. If he or she blinked an eye, the picture would be blurred.

1. You can conclude that
   a. friends thought of Lincoln as lively and happy.
   b. Lincoln was sad and gloomy.
   c. photos show us just what Lincoln looked like.
   d. Lincoln never smiled.

2. There are no action-packed sports photos from Lincoln's time. Which fact supports that conclusion?
   a. Lincoln was the most photographed person.
   b. Sports were just as popular then as now.
   c. Lincoln's expression changed when he spoke.
   d. The person photographed had to hold still for several seconds.

3. Which conclusion does the main idea suggest?
   a. Few people knew Lincoln well.
   b. Photographs influence our idea of Lincoln.
   c. Photography was Lincoln's favorite hobby.
   d. Most presidents prefer serious photos.

4. Cameras in Lincoln's time weren't as good as they are now. Underline the sentence that supports that conclusion.

Practice Exercise *16*

Our ancestors believed the sea was a river surrounding the soil on which they lived. Therefore, they named the planet Earth. If they had known what the planet was really like, they may have named it differently. Most of it is covered with water.

In our group of planets, Earth is unique. It has many oceans. They exist because their surface temperatures range from about 28°F (–2°C) in the polar regions to about 86°F (30°C) in the tropics. Within that temperature range, most of the water remains liquid. Above that range, water boils; below it freezes.

All forms of life need water. It dissolves more substances than any other liquid. To live, all life forms must break down chemicals. They must take in water to do many tasks such as digest food. Water supports life in other ways as well. For example, it stores heat. The seas absorb heat in summer. They release it in winter.

1. If the surface temperature rose too high then
   a. the oceans would boil away.
   b. new life forms would begin.
   c. ice would spread from the poles.
   d. all the water would freeze.

2. Winters would be colder if there were no oceans. Which fact supports that conclusion?
   a. All life forms must break down chemicals.
   b. Water dissolves substances.
   c. Water helps digest food.
   d. The seas store and release heat.

3. Which conclusion does the main idea of the first paragraph suggest?
   a. Our planet could be called Ocean.
   b. People thought the sea was a narrow river.
   c. Earth is unique in our group of planets.
   d. Our ancestors named the planet Earth.

4. You can conclude that cactus plants need water. Underline the sentence that supports that conclusion.

— Practice Exercise **17** ——

Hollywood is the center of American films. However, the industry wasn't born there. It began in New Jersey.

The industry's move west began in 1910. Al Christie was then chief director for Centaur Pictures. He made Westerns. It was hard to make New Jersey look like the Wild West. He thought California would be better. Centaur's owner, David Horsley, disagreed. He thought Florida would be better. They agreed to flip a coin. If Christie won, they'd move to the West. If Horsley won, they'd move to the South. Christie won.

He went to California to look for sites. At last, he found an old building in Hollywood. It was large and cheap. In 1911, Centaur made it the company's studio.

Hollywood began to bloom. Soon fifteen other film companies set up studios there. Sunshine and scenic areas made filming easy. No longer did movie cowboys ride the ranges of New Jersey.

1. You can conclude that
   a. the taxes in New Jersey were too high.
   b. Westerns were Centaur's most important movies.
   c. Al Christie had been brought up in California.
   d. Horsley was bitterly disappointed.

2. Christie concluded that California would be a good place to make movies. What fact supported that conclusion?
   a. Fifteen other film companies were already there.
   b. All their equipment would have to be moved.
   c. Florida is closer to New Jersey.
   d. Sunny weather made filming easy.

3. Which conclusion does the main idea suggest?
   a. Centaur Pictures is no longer in business.
   b. Florida was the film capital for a while.
   c. Movie companies are moving to New Jersey.
   d. A coin toss made Hollywood the film capital.

4. Both Christie and Horsley wanted a place with warm weather. Underline the sentences that support that conclusion.

— Practice Exercise 18 —

Marie Curie's childhood should have been ideal. What more could she ask than to be born to loving parents? They understood her and supported her talents in science and math. But the clouds that were to shadow Marie's life soon rolled onto her horizon. As a young girl, she learned that life was hard and, at times, unfair. To achieve her dreams she would have to be patient, strong, and determined.

Marie faced her first hardship when she was still a child. Her mother developed tuberculosis. The child could not understand why her mother did not kiss her. She wondered why her mother used special dishes. Hard to bear, too, was her mother's long stay in a French hospital. Yet it did help to prepare Marie for the final separation. Her mother died before Marie was eleven years old.

1. You can conclude that Marie's mother did not kiss her daughter because she
   a. didn't understand the child.
   b. was afraid of giving her tuberculosis.
   c. disliked Marie.
   d. feared that Marie would give her a cold.

2. You can conclude that Marie's mother died
   a. when Marie was ten.
   b. at a very young age.
   c. after Marie's eleventh birthday.
   d. at home.

3. Which conclusion does the main idea suggest?
   a. Marie Curie's childhood was a sad one.
   b. Tuberculosis is not very dangerous.
   c. Marie Curie was afraid of her mother.
   d. French hospitals were not well run in Marie Curie's day.

4. Marie's parents made sure that she had a good education. Underline the sentence that supports that conclusion.

Practice Exercise *19*

Sylvester Graham spent much of his life fighting what he thought was a deadly enemy. He loathed white bread. As far back as 1830, he felt that such processed foods were low in nutrients. He urged people to eat coarse-grained bread and cereals instead. Ill for years, Graham started a strict diet in middle age. He spoke out against spicy foods. He urged people to try meatless meals. He promoted bathing and exercise. He even urged people to brush their teeth. Some people thought such ideas were wacky. Many thought Graham was a strange man.

The enemy of white bread was a pioneer of sorts. One of his followers created the first cold breakfast cereal. He called it *Granula.* Perhaps the greatest of Graham's legacies was the cracker he developed. It is, of course, made of whole wheat flour. It is *not* made with white flour.

1. You can conclude that Graham would have considered doughnuts and chili
   a. bad foods.
   b. the perfect way to start the day.
   c. high in nutrients.
   d. better than *Granula.*

2. Which of Graham's ideas still seems wacky today?
   a. Eating less meat is healthful.
   b. Brushing your teeth is wise.
   c. Exercise helps keep you healthy.
   d. Spicy foods aren't healthful.

3. Which conclusion does the main idea suggest?
   a. Graham's ideas were foolish.
   b. Graham crackers are the perfect breakfast food.
   c. Graham's ideas were ahead of their time.
   d. Graham was an amusing man.

4. You can conclude that Graham favored meals made with vegetables. Underline the sentence that supports that conclusion.

— Practice Exercise **20** —

When one thinks of North America at the turn of the century, colorful images come to mind. Picture the ornate parlor with flickering gaslights. See the happy riders in a horse-drawn buggy. Watch the ladies dancing at a ball in fancy, tightly laced dresses. Life was grand—for some.

For others, it was a time of stress. The nation was sliding out of its worst economic depression to date. A third of the railroads had failed. Thousands of businesses and banks had closed. In big cities and small towns hundreds of thousands went without jobs. Few were spared hardship. Not long before, the United States and Canada had been rural nations of small farms and hand-produced goods. Now manufacturing had become king.

1. People who only knew how to make goods by hand didn't get work in factories because
a. they didn't have the right skills.
b. they went on working by hand.
c. they moved to farms.
d. people still got around by horse-drawn buggy.

2. If hundreds of thousands had no jobs, then they
a. could buy railroad tickets to find work.
b. could put money into the bank each week.
c. might save money to buy a buggy.
d. had no money to buy what others made.

3. Which conclusion does the main idea suggest about the turn of the century?
a. It was a time when life was grand for all.
b. It was a romantic time of flickering gaslights.
c. It was the best and worst of times in North America.
d. It was a time of stress for all.

4. The author thinks that people like to remember good times and forget bad times. Circle the paragraph that supports that conclusion.

PART FIVE

Writing Activities

The writing activities that follow will help you draw conclusions. The activities will also help you use conclusions when you write.

Follow the directions. Then answer each question carefully. Sometimes your teacher may ask you to work alone. Sometimes he or she may ask you to work with other students.

You will need to write your answers on separate paper. Your teacher may ask you to write those answers in a notebook or journal. Then all your writing activities will be in the same place.

The activities in each book get harder as you go along. Look back at the activity you have already finished before you begin a new one. If you have questions about drawing conclusions, reread the lessons in Parts One and Two (pages 5–16).

Writing Activity 1

Read the following passage from *The Story of an Eye-Witness* by Jack London. The eye-witness reports on the devastation of the San Francisco earthquake

By Wednesday afternoon, inside of twelve hours, half of the heart of the city was gone. At that time I watched the vast fire from out on the bay. It was dead calm. Not a flicker of wind stirred. Yet from every side wind was pouring in upon the city. East, west, north, and south, strong winds were blowing upon the doomed city. The heated air rising made an enormous suck. Thus did the fire of itself build its own colossal chimney through the atmosphere. Day and night this dead calm continued, and yet, near the flames, the wind was often half a gale, so mighty was the suck.

Wednesday night saw the destruction of the very heart of the city. Dynamite was lavishly used, and many of San Francisco's proudest structures were crumbled into ruins by man himself, but there was no withstanding the onrush of flames. Time and again successful stands were made by the fire fighters, but every time the flames flanked around on either side, or came up from the rear, they turned the hard-won victory to defeat.

Complete each of the following sentences by drawing a conclusion that makes sense. Remember, a conclusion is a decision you make that is based on the facts you have read.

1. The eye-witness describes the sights of San Francisco. From this description, you can conclude that San Francisco was

_____.

2. The passages tells about the wind and the fire. From this description, you can conclude that the fire was

_____.

3. Dynamite was used in the heart of the city. From the passage, you can conclude that it was used to

_____.

Share your answers with another student in your class. Did you both draw the same conclusions? How are your answers the same? How are they different?

Writing Activity 2

Read the following passage from "The Open Window" by Saki. The main character, Framton Nuttel, goes to the country to recover from a bad case of nerves.

"My aunt will be down presently, Mr. Nuttel," said a very self-possessed young lady of fifteen. "In the meantime you must try to put up with me."

Framton Nuttel endeavored to say the correct something which should duly flatter the niece of the moment without unduly discounting the aunt that was to come. Privately he doubted more than ever whether these formal visits on a succession of total strangers would do much toward helping the nerve cure which he was supposed to be undergoing. . . .

"Do you know many of the people round here?" asked the niece, when she judged that they had had sufficient silent communion.

"Hardly a soul," said Framton. . . .

"Then you know practically nothing about my aunt?" pursued the self-possessed young lady.

A.   Answer each of the following questions. Write your answers on a separate piece of paper or in your writing notebook. Your teacher may ask you to talk about your answers with the class.

1. What can you conclude about the young niece Mr. Nuttel met? What words support your conclusion?

2. How would you define *case of nerves?*

3. Why would a person whose is suffering from a case of nerves go to visit a stranger?

B.   Think of meeting someone for the first time or being a stranger in a new town or school. What kind of things could you do to be less nervous? How could you meet new people and make friends?

Make a list of your ideas. Write your list on a separate piece of paper or in your writing notebook. Then use your list to help you write a paragraph about your plan of action.

Writing Activity 3

Read the following poem "The Snow Storm" by Ralph
Waldo Emerson.

The Snow Storm

Announced by all the trumpets of the sky,

Arrives the snow, and driving o'er the fields,

Seems nowhere to alight: the whited air.

Hides hills and woods, the river and the heaven,

And veils the farm-house at the garden's end.

The sled and the traveller stopped, the courier's feet

Delayed, all friends shut out, the housemates sit

Around the radiant fireplace, enclosed

In a tumultuous privacy of storm.

A.   Answer each of the following questions. Write your
answers on a separate piece of paper or in your writing
notebook. Your teacher may ask you to talk about your
answers with the class.

1. What signaled the arrival of the snow? What conclusions can you
draw about the landscape? Explain your answer.

2. What problems has the snow caused? Why would traveling in
snow be difficult? Use details from the poem to support your
conclusions.

B. What do you think it would be like to be out in a snowstorm? What challenges would you face? What kind of clothing would you need? Would you need other supplies? Write your ideas on a separate piece of paper or in your writing notebook. Then write a short paragraph about your experience in the snowstorm. Use your list of ideas to help you.

Writing Activity 4

Read the following paragraph about Angela.

> Angela hid behind the door. She heard everything the strange man said. As she listened to him talk, Angela felt angrier and angrier. I must stop him, she thought. And I will!

What happens next? Who is the strange man? Why is Angela listening to him? What conclusions can you draw about Angela? Is she brave or afraid? What will happen when she meets the strange man?

Write your ideas on a separate piece of paper or in your writing notebook. Then use your list to help you write a short paragraph about Angela. The paragraph should be at least five sentences long.

Writing Activity **5**

Read the following passage about Mark and his visit to
grandfather's farm.

Mark was at his grandfather's farm for a visit.

"Why don't you go out and pick some apples?" his
grandfather suggested. "The apples aren't quite ripe, and we
shouldn't eat them yet, but they'll be good in applesauce."

Mark loved apples—even green ones—so he spent all
afternoon picking them. Of course, he couldn't stop
himself from eating one now and then. By the end of
the afternoon, Mark realized he had eaten six apples.
Suddenly, Mark raced back to the house.

Answer each of the following questions. Write your
answers on a separate piece of paper or in your writing
notebook. Your teacher may ask you to talk about your
answers with the class.

1. Why did Grandfather tell Mark to pick the apples even
   though he knew they were not ripe? What conclusions
   can you draw from the passage?

2. What kind of person was Mark? Did he seem helpful and hard
   working? What conclusions can you draw from the passage?
   Explain your answer.

3. Why did Mark go back to the house suddenly? Write your
   conclusion and list the details from the passage that support
   your conclusions.

Writing Activity 6

Read the following passage "The Cicada and the Ants" adapted from Aesop.

The cicada was happy and content as he sat and sang on a leaf. He could not understand why the ants worked so hard, even in summer.

"Carrying grain in this heat! How crazy!"

Time passed and winter arrived. One day the hungry cicada came to the ants while they were happily eating their grain.

"Will you give me some of your grain? You have so much!"

"But why didn't you put some away last summer?" they replied.

"I didn't have time," answered the cicada. "I had to sing."

"If you sang in the summer, then you can dance in the winter!" said the ants, laughing.

A. Answer each of the following questions. Write your answers on a separate piece of paper or in your writing notebook. Your teacher may ask you to talk about your answers with the class.

1. Why did the ants work all day in the summer sun? What conclusions can you draw from the passage?

2. What characteristics would you use to describe the behavior of the cicada? of the ants? What conclusions can you draw from the passage?

3. What did the ants mean when they said, "If you sang in the summer, then you can dance in the winter"? Explain your answer.

   B. What lesson was the author trying to teach? Do you know ways to apply that lesson? Write your ideas on a separate piece of paper or in your writing notebook. Then write a short paragraph about your interpretation of the lesson. The paragraph should be at least five sentences long. Use your list of ideas to help you.

Writing Activity 7

Read the following passage about Sandy and her favorite school class and activity.

Of all the classes that Sandy took in school, she loved art class the most. She would spend all her free time drawing and painting.

"Your artwork is very special," her art teacher told her. "I've never had a student who is as good as you are."

Sandy smiled with pleasure. She loved to paint the mountains, the blue sky with its fluffy clouds, the trees and flowers, and all the things in nature.

When the yearly art contest came, Sandy entered her very best painting. Finally, the day arrived when the prizes were given. Sandy was the happiest person on Earth.

A. Answer each of the following questions. Write your answers on a separate piece of paper or in your writing notebook. Your teacher may ask you to talk about your answers with the class.

1. Did the art teacher compliment or criticize Sandy's art? Explain your answer.

2. Some artists paint very modern pictures. Some artists paint animals, some paint scenery, and some paint people. What kind of pictures did Sandy like to paint? What conclusions can you draw from the passage?

3. What do you think happened when the prizes were awarded? Write your conclusion and list the details from the passage that support your conclusions.